St.-Louis-du-Ha!-Ha!, QC

the Book of
Canadian Epitaphs

NANCY MILLAR

BRINDLE & GLASS

Copyright © Nancy Millar 2004

All rights reserved. The use of any part of this
publication reproduced, transmitted in any form or
by any means, electronic, mechanical, recording or
otherwise, or stored in a retrieval system, without
the prior consent of the publisher is an infringement
of the copyright law. In the case of photocopying
or other reprographic copying of the material, a
licence must be obtained from the Canadian
Reprography Collective before proceeding.

National Library of Canada Cataloguing in Publication
Millar, Nancy
The final word : the book of Canadian epitaphs /
Nancy Millar

ISBN 0-9732481-4-9

1. Epitaphs—Canada. I. Title.

PN6291.M54 2004   929'.5   C2004-900715-7

Photos: Nancy Millar

Brindle & Glass Publishing
www.brindleandglass.com

1   2   3   4   5   07   06   05   04

PRINTED AND BOUND IN CANADA

*To all the people who have
tramped through graveyards with me,
and especially to my husband Bruce,
who has done more than most!*

Ingersoll, ON

**Let's sit upon the ground
and talk of graves
and worms
and epitaphs
and tell sad stories of the death of kings.**

From Richard III by William Shakespeare

People often ask me why I explore graveyards. Am I, they wonder, just a little bit morbid perhaps? A little odd perhaps? So I put on my most reasonable expression and tell them, reasonably, that I am doing exactly what I should be doing. I am remembering those who came before me. Why else do we erect tombstones out there in the graveyard? Why else do we put names and dates and loving messages upon the stones if not to mark the lives that came before ours? It's that simple. I am doing what I am supposed to be doing. I am remembering.

Mind you, I am also recording the words and symbols on many of those graves. Together, they tell an amazing story of Canada and the way we were. We're an interesting bunch, we Canadians, not that we often know that fact, let alone admit it. But I'm here to tell you that, thanks to my graveyard research, I know that Canadians are just as goofy, interesting, bloody, jealous, loving, noble, nasty, vengeful, long-suffering, etc., etc., as any other people. The proof is in the graveyard.

Don't be offended by my sometimes lighthearted approach. I respect those who have come before, but I take the advice on a gravemarker in the Millarville, Alberta, cemetery. Kathleen Sharpe's marker says, "Sit with me until the shadows go; then smile."

Isn't that wonderful advice? I love those words. I wish I had put them over my dad. He liked to sit at our kitchen window and watch his trees, the trees along the creek beside our house. He'd watch the wind blowing through them, the light dancing among them, and then he'd smile. They represented so much—his successful emigration to a new country, his own farm, his very own land, a good house, things he could never have hoped for in the old country. But one day, during his descent into Alzheimers, he forgot his trees. He looked around at them and said to my brother, "I think I should know those trees." But he didn't anymore and we knew it was time for the nursing home. He couldn't smile anymore and neither could we right then. But time passes and we visit him in the cemetery now and smile. There on a standard black granite grave marker is his name and the epitaph, "Life's work well done." It's a common epitaph but it is meaningful to us and makes us remember.

So come with me to the graveyard. It's not scary. It's just us. We're often solemn out there, often silent, but every now and then the words on our grave markers reveal the world we have come from. It's actually history, but I hesitate to put that word in the same breath as graveyards, lest I be considered too weird for anything, so let me just say this book contains epitaphs. Happy funny ones, sad forlorn ones, big-name ones, no-name ones, old ones, new ones. All of them Canadian, all of them us.

Please walk on the grass.

> Thomas Thompson, 1913–1985
> Mount Pleasant Cemetery, Toronto, ON

After retiring as Toronto's Parks Commissioner, "Tommy" Thompson led tours through the Mount Pleasant Cemetery and always encouraged people to walk upon the grass that had been under his care for so many years. Thus the choice of words on his gravemarker.

This wasn't my idea.

KRAIG HANCOCKS, 1955–1996
TAPPEN CEMETERY, NEAR SALMON ARM, BC

There is no beating around the bush in this modern epitaph, although it contains about the same message as some of the old-fashioned ones that mentioned "God's will" in connection with death. Only the words change.

I told you I was sick

Constance, b. 1928, and William Fedora, 1919–1993
St. Stephen Ukrainian Orthodox Cemetery,
Pleasant Home, MB

This epitaph is always mentioned whenever amusing grave words are discussed, but it's not so easy to find. People, or their descendants, tend to decide upon more sedate and traditional epitaphs when the time comes.

All things considered:
We'd rather be in Philadelphia

Gladys Limpert, 1909–1989
Delia, AB, Cemetery

It was W. C. Fields, the American humorist, who joked that he wanted the words, "On the whole, I'd rather be in Philadelphia" over his grave. Since then, versions of his epitaph have often been used, but Fields himself is buried in Hollywood without any words—just his name and dates. We Canadians are not big on humour in the graveyard, no matter how gentle it is, but it's a lovely surprise when it appears.

> You'll never see a Loomis car
> Following a hearse.
>
> C. W. O. Louis Martel, 1927–1977
> Edmonton, AB, Cemetery

In other words, you can't take it with you—your money, that is!

> Be valiant to the end,
> Be true.
>
> — MACKAY FAMILY GRAVES
> FERNHILL CEMETERY, SAINT JOHN, NB

Imagine being told to be "valiant" nowadays, or "true," for that matter. Some of the lovely noble words have gone out of fashion, regrettably.

> **"Be Good To One Another."**
>
> — DUNCAN MCINTYRE FERGUSON, 1885–1913
> NORTH BAY, ON, CEMETERY

Apparently, these were young Duncan's last words, so his family chose to use them as his epitaph. He was, according to the Ferguson family cairn, "North Bay's first born citizen."

> I'll meet you when my chores are through,
> And between now and then
> Till I see you again
> I'll be lov'n you. . . . Love me.
>
> ESTHER CZEMERES, 1914–1992
FORT QU'APPELLE, SK, CEMETERY

Two favourite Canadian epitaphs are "Ever Loved, Ever Remembered," and "Gone But Not Forgotten." That seems to be about as much emotion as we are able to declare publicly. However, there are lovely exceptions. The one above uses the words of a popular western song often sung by Wilf Carter in the 1940s and 1950s.

She loved, was loved, and died.

NELLIE CHAPMAN, DIED 1935
VERNON, BC, CEMETERY

Certainly no unnecessary mush in this epitaph, but all the elements are there—she loved and was loved and who can ask for anything more?

Vernon, BC

In memory of
Malcolm McQuaig, who
Departed this life Aug. 9th, 1817,
Aged 41 years, who left a Duti-
full Wife and Four Affectionate
Children. Also
Margery his Widow who
after the Death of her said
Husband was Weded to
David Kenady Clark.
She Departed this life Feb. 7th,
1833 in the 45th year of her
Age she left only two of her
First Husbands Children
And Four of the Later
To Lament Their Loss.

Laurel Hill Cemetery, Pictou, NS

Never mind sentimental messages of love and all that stuff. Instead, here's one of the most complete explanations ever found in a graveyard of husbands and wife and the complications thereof.

> If I could do one thing alone,
> a verse, or prayer of lasting worth,
> I'd seek St. Stephen's gentle slope
> and carve there the words
> "I Love You!"
>
> MARJORIE EDITH SHAW, 1912–1985
> ST. STEPHEN'S ANGLICAN CEMETERY, VICTORIA, BC

St. Stephen's is a lovely country graveyard and this epitaph is a lovely exception to the usual matter-of-fact messages on women's graves.

> By the grace of God she
> excelled as a woman
> as a wife and as a Mother
> and finished her course with joy.
> Her memory is blessed.
>
> ANN STRANG, DIED 1837
> CAMBRIDGE, ON, CEMETERY

It's heartwarming to see Ann receive such a fulsome message, but there's a grave next to hers that tells us one David Strang was born in 1837. Reading between the lines, it's likely poor Ann died in childbirth, a fate that was common in the bad old days.

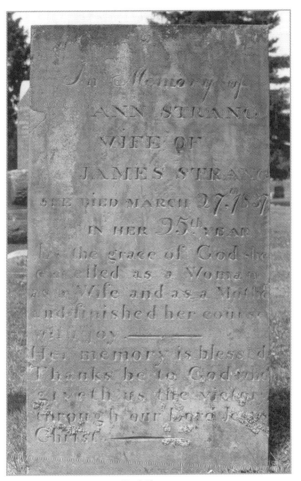

Cambridge, ON

> Goodbye, good bye, Dear Husband
> Entrusted to your care
> Is left our infant child until
> In Heaven I meet you there.
>
> CATHERINE SHEAHAN, 1849–1875
ST. STEPHEN'S CEMETERY, OLD CHELSEA, QC

Again, this woman probably died in childbirth. In fact, the epitaph almost says so—almost, but not quite.

> Sacred to the Memory of Jane,
> Wife of Robert Hiscock
> who died in Child-birth.
> In the midst of life,
> we are in death.

Jane Hiscock, Died 1830
Trinity, NL, Cemetery

This is one of the rare times that the word 'childbirth' is mentioned directly on a gravestone. Usually, you have to winkle out the fact by checking dates and ages on nearby graves.

> I would have lent thee wings, dear heart
> Even though it put us worlds apart
> But wild the wings and wild the heart
> That could us in death now part.
>
> FRANK RUSSELL "RUSS" BAKER, 1910–1958
> ON A CAIRN NEAR FORT ST. JAMES, BC

In the interests of gender equality, above is a thoughtful tribute from a wife to her husband, a bush pilot who crashed near the site of the cairn.

> If Tears Could Build A
> Stairway, And Memories
> A Lane, I'd Walk Right Up
> To Heaven And Bring
> You Home Again.
>
> GEORGE KENNETH HARROLD, 1951–1974
> FORT NELSON, BC, CEMETERY

Another loving message for a man, also in northern Canada. Maybe we can express more emotion in the graveyards of the North?

Whom we have loved and lost awhile

WILLIAM DENNIS RATCLIFF, 1928–1979
SUNDRE, AB, CEMETERY

In just a few words, this original epitaph manages to convey regret, love, and the hope of reunion.

To be continued.

LORREN TAYLOR, 1907–1987
RED DEER, AB, CEMETERY

Another brief and original epitaph. About this one, Mrs. Taylor explained that she spent a long time thinking about just the right words for her husband, and this is what she came up with. It suggests a life after death without getting specific about the details.

Wm Pierce.
Died Feb 31, 1860.
Aged 73 years.

ST. MARY MAGDALENE CEMETERY, PICTON, ON

Mr. Pierce is known as the man who never died because there is no February 31. His grave is often sought out by tourists.

Picton, ON

Margaret McEdward
Born in the evening of the
22 Nov. 1850.
Died on the morning of the
31 Aug. 1871.
Also
In memory of her two infant sisters

South Lancaster, ON, Cemetery

This is another epitaph concerned with time. Surprisingly, the man who should have reference to time on his gravemarker does not. Sir Sandford Fleming, the inventor of time zones, is buried in Beechwood Cemetery, Ottawa, without a murmur about his part in organizing time around the world. His marker says simply, "Born January 7, 1827; Married January 3, 1855; Died July 22, 1915."

> In memory of George
> Died May 2, 1851, age 32.
> Eldest son of Andrew Clephane Esq.
> Late Sheriff of Fifeshire, Scotland

GEORGE CLEPHANE
FERGUS, ON, CEMETERY

Epitaphs leave out so much. This one tells us only that George came from Scotland and died young in Canada. It doesn't hint at the fact that George's death far from home inspired his sister to write a poem about her unhappy brother, the words of which eventually became the well-known hymn, "There Were Ninety and Nine."

Suddenly
Sunday noon
April 3, 1892
Mary Smith,
Beloved wife of
Walter Grose,
Aged 39 years.
Led an earthly choir in the morning,
And sang as her solo in the anthem,
"Angels to Beckon Me Nearer My God To Thee,"
She joined the heavenly choir
an hour
afterwards.
"She hath done what she could."

MARY SMITH, 1853–1892
MOUNT ROYAL CEMETERY, MONTREAL, QC

It has been suggested by modern wags that Mary should have picked a different hymn, one with words a little less specific, more like the words of "There Were Ninety and Nine" perhaps. Incidentally, the expression "She hath done what she could" is high praise in the Christian context. It is not as grudging as it sounds.

He did his bit.

PTE. ALEX IRELAND, C. E. F., 1876–1928
MOOSE JAW, SK, CEMETERY

This too seems a bit stingy in its praise, but the expression is used fairly often to convey the idea that the deceased did his or her best in the course of their lives.

> Make no small plans,
> They hold no magic to stir men's blood.
>
> SENATOR DONALD CAMERON, 1901–1989
> AND HIS WIFE STELLA MARY CAMERON, 1900–1982
> BANFF, AB, CEMETERY

The graves in the Banff cemetery are dwarfed by the towering Rocky Mountains on all sides—what better place from which to advise the living to make big plans?

In loving memory of
Forest and Maud Kidney

>Died 1979 and 1977 respectively
>Banff, AB, Cemetery

These stones have naturally become known as the Kidney Stones of the Banff cemetery.

> **It's not that I am always right**
> **It's just that I am never wrong.**
>
> HOWARD STOUGHTON, 1926–1987
> BARRYVALE, ON, CEMETERY

Apparently, Mr. Stoughton used this expression all the time. Thus it was decided to let him say it over and over again in the graveyard.

> We cannot tell who next
> May fall beneath thy
> Chastening rod. One must
> Be first but let us all
> Prepare to meet our God.
>
> — Mary Ann Pollock, 1879–1903
> Sintaluta, SK, Cemetery

This is an epitaph in the "warning" genre. Often these warning stones included carvings of death's heads, bony fingers, empty eye sockets, etc.—the equivalent of modern advertising. "Get thee to a church before it's too late" would be the message intended.

> **Whoſe unaffected piety**
> **Peculiar Dignity**
> ** Serenity of Temper and**
> **Benevolence of Heart**
> **Rendered her juſtly and**
> **Univerſally Beloved and Reſpected**
> **In her Lateſt Hour.**
>
> HANNAH WINSLOW, DIED 1796
> OLD BURYING GROUND, FREDERICTON, NB

On very early gravestones, the *s* is often written as an *f*. Hannah's is a good example of such graves, when the words used were generous and noble.

The Maritimes had a number of well-known gravestone sculptors in the 1700s and 1800s who loved to add warnings to the biographical information and the images already on the marker. Thus, you'll find across the top of a gravemarker such lines as

> O Look on this stone, ye careless
> Trim your lamp and be sober.

Or

> Be Ye Also Ready.

Or

> Death is a Debt that Must be Paid.

If those words weren't enough to convince you to prepare, how about these, which were the favourites of "J. W.", a Nova Scotia sculptor?

> Life is Uncertain, Tyrant Death Approaches
>
> The Judge is at the Door, Prepare to meet Your God

> In memory of Peter Pennington, Coloured
> Born in Maryland about AD 1827,
> Died at Sarnia, 18th Sept. 1884.
> He followed here for 25 years
> the calling of fisherman.
> Having no child or known relative,
> bequeathed his small bequest
> of about $1000
> in equal portions to the several
> charities of the town.
>
> PETER PENNINGTON, 1827–1884
> SARNIA, ON, CEMETERY

There are several remarkable features of this gravemarker. First of all, the word "coloured" seldom appears on gravemarkers. And secondly, $1000 was a lot of money in 1884. Mr. Pennington certainly "did his bit," to use that other old tombstone remark.

> A little flower of love
> That blossomed but to die
> Transplanted now above
> To bloom with God on high

MARTHA ALLEN, DIED 1872
AGED 4 MONTHS AND 26 DAYS
UNION CEMETERY, OSHAWA, ON

Epitaphs for children in days gone by often gave the child's exact age at death, right down to the day. Also, their epitaphs were often couched in gardening metaphors.

Today we bloom, tomorrow die.

> Joseph Bartlett, Died 1871
> Brigus, NL, Cemetery

However, while a gardening metaphor for a child mourns an early loss of life, this gardening reference for an adult is matter-of-fact and accepting.

Another common epitaph in the gardening mode starts out with the question, "Who cut this flower?" "The Master did," the next line explains.

> Ah, that's the reason a bird can sing
> On his darkest day.
> He believes in spring.
>
> Eva Leona Hedges Miller, 1885–1970
Olds, AB, Cemetery

Seasons are also a favourite subject for epitaphs, spring in this case representing new life, new beginnings.

> **Short spring, early autumn.**
>
> For son of Rev. Norman Macleod,
Pictou, NS, Cemetery

Again, seasons are used to indicate lifespan. There are only four words in this epitaph, but they say so much.

> Here lies
> Petter D. Brodair
> in his last and best bedroom
>
> Petter D. Brodair
St. James Anglican Cemetery, Pictou, NS

It might be an epitaph myth, but it is said that Petter Brodair moved a lot and was never happy with his accommodation. Thus the reference to his "last and best bedroom" could be a secular one. Or it could refer to the expectation of better things in the next world.

> First white child born on
> Niagara Frontier Sept. 26, 1786
> 8 d'ys after her parents walked
> From New Jersey to Bender farm

REBECCA G. BIGGAR, 1786–1880
LUNDY'S LANE CEMETERY, NIAGARA FALLS, ON

Epitaphs often contain information about the "first" and the "last." The "first postmaster," the "last British soldier," that sort of thing. However, we are moving away from references to the first "white" person to settle in the district or the first "white" woman born in a certain region and so on.

The last survivor of General Custer

JOHN MCALPINE, 1849–1941
THREE HILLS, AB, CEMETERY

History tells us there were no soldiers who survived the famous Battle of the Little Big Horn, so what is this claim on McAlpine's stone? Turns out he was with the Seventh Cavalry but his supply wagons got stuck on the way there, so he missed the big battle. Thus, he was able to claim he "survived."

Three Hills, AB

"The Last of the Muleskinners"

Harold Huntington Phillips, 1896–1988
Dalemead, AB, Cemetery

Another example of our interest in who came first and what's on second! Baddeck, Nova Scotia, has a very important "first" mentioned in its cemetery on the gravestone of John Alexander Douglas McCurdy, 1886–1961. The information includes mention of all the honourary titles he received through his distinguished aviation and political careers, but the top line is the important one. It says,

> First British Subject to Fly in the British Empire, February 23, 1909.

> Weep not for me now,
> Weep for me never
> For I'm going to do
> nothing for ever & ever.

> HARRIET ELIZABETH CONNELL, 1898–1989
> OKOTOKS, AB, CEMETERY

This lovely bit of whimsy is known as the Tired Woman's Epitaph. The lines above are the last two lines of a much longer version:

> Here lies a poor woman who always was tired
> For she lived in a place where help wasn't hired
> Her last words on earth were, Dear friends I am going
> Where washing ain't done nor sweeping nor sewing
> And everything there is exact to my wishes,
> For there they don't eat and there's no washing of dishes . . .

> Sleep on, sweet babe
> And take thy rest.
> God called thee home,
> He thought it best.

FREDDY SHEPPARD, DIED AUG. 1905, AGED 6 MONTHS
WETASKIWIN, AB, CEMETERY

This epitaph for a child was common in earlier days. It was double comfort for a grieving family that the babe now "slept" and was at "home" with God.

> How much sorrow,
> how much joy,
> Is buried with a
> darling boy.

EDWIN LEBEUF, AGED 4 YEARS, NO DATES
MISSION CEMETERY, NEAR SPIRIT RIVER, AB

These words were found on a grave in an abandoned mission cemetery in the Peace River country of Alberta, the words still crying out on a heart-shaped white marker.

near Spirit River, AB

Walk softly for a Dream lies buried here.

People's Cemetery, Charlottetown, PEI

T'is only a grave but O have care
For world wide hopes lie buried here,
And ye do not know how deep a shade
This simple grave in our home hath made.

Catherine Anderson, 1849–1870
Ormstown, QC, Cemetery

Sometimes old-fashioned words can express grief so well, especially when it's young people that they mourn.

> I want to be an angel
> And with the angels stand,
> A crown upon my forehead,
> A harp within my hand;
> There right before my Saviour
> So glorious and so bright
> I'd wake the sweetest music
> And praise Him day and night.
>
> JANE TOWNSEND, 1859–1868
> WAKEFIELD, QC, CEMETERY

In the top curve of this old marble marker are the words, "Heaven is my home," as if the Townsends are making doubly sure that their daughter is "taken home" in the Christian context.

> For he comes, the human child,
> To the waters and the wild
> With a faery, hand in hand,
> From a world more full of
> Weeping than he can
> understand.
>
> Michael Coyne, 1947–1983
Queen's Park Cemetery, Calgary, AB

This is a quote from William Yeats' poem, "The Stolen Child." Yeats is himself well-known for his gravemarker in the Drumcliffe graveyard in Ireland, which says simply,

> Cast a cold eye
> On life, on death
> Horseman, pass by.

> **It is so soon that I am done**
> **I wonder why I was begun**
>
> Kory Dale Marshall, 1969–1971
Delia, AB, Cemetery

Sometimes this sad little verse is preceded by the lines:

> Ope'd my eyes, took a peep
> Didn't like it, went to sleep.

> Alas, alas, my son, my son,
> I saw him sail to the strangers' land
> Where nought remained for me
> But the tearful eye and a heartfelt sigh
> And I gaze on the dark blue sea
> But now he lies in the strangers' land,
> Cold cold as they could be,
> It found him a death and a green green grave
> And a broken heart for me.
>
> Samuel Begley, 1845–1870
> United Church Cemetery, Aylwin, QC

Speaking of broken-hearted, this is the tribute of parents who saw their son leave for Canada to make a new life. Instead, he found "a green green grave."

> Each man stood at his post
> While all the weaker ones
> Went by and showed once
> More to all the world
> How Englishmen should die.
>
> Everett Edward Elliott
Died on duty on the Titanic, April 15, 1912
Fairview Cemetery, Halifax, NS

Once again, it must be parents who remember a son with these noble words. How else could you make sense of such a sudden terrible tragedy?

In memory of Agnes,
Relict of Francis Longworth, Esq.
Endeared to her family
By her affectionate disposition
And Christian deportment
She has left her children
Five sons and five daughters
To mourn the loss of a tender parent.

Agnes Longworth, 1775–1850
Charlottetown, PEI, Cemetery

In this epitaph, it's the children's turn to mourn for a parent and they have used lovely words to do so. Incidentally, "relict" simply means "widow."

"Tell mother I'll be all right in the morning."

> JOHN REGINALD THORNE, DIED 1910
> MOUNT PLEASANT CEMETERY, TORONTO, ON

Again, this is a message to a parent. John's horse fell on him during a military exercise and as he was carried off the field, these were his last words.

Do Not Resurrect

Roy William Devore, 1891–1969
Mount Pleasant Cemetery, Edmonton, AB

It's unusual to find this kind of message in a graveyard. Generally, the opposite is found—the hope in a life after death.

Give strength to my children

> Annie Iron Red Crow, 1902–1983
> St. Catherine's Cemetery, Standoff, AB

Safe in the arms of the grandfathers

> Keysoos McLean Shirt, 1987–1988
> Fort Vermilion, AB, Cemetery

These are two messages from native graveyards, one offering advice, the other offering comfort.

Big Jack has gone upstairs

> BIG JACK, 1898–1969
> EDAM, SK, CEMETERY

The summit attained

> ANDREW S. SIBBALD, 1888–1945
> BANFF, AB, CEMETERY

She faltered by the wayside
And the angels took her home.

> DAISY SUMNER, 1877–1883
> YALE, BC, CEMETERY

Explicit references to death are often avoided on grave-markers, with some rather lovely results. Take "faltered by the wayside" in the third example. Somehow it seems kinder for a six-year-old.

Edam, SK

I heard the owl call my name.

John Donald McDonald, 1922–1990
St. Stephen's Anglican Cemetery, Victoria, BC

In most loving memory of our darling
"Scottie"
Eric Grant Mackay
Who joined the noble
Army of Martyrs
and entered into rest eternal

Eric Grant Mackay, Died 1902
Union Cemetery, Calgary, AB

Again, words referring directly to death do not appear in either the modern epitaph (top) or the old-fashioned one following. Common euphemisms include "Sleeping," "Gone Home," "Promoted," and "At Rest."

> When the final summons comes
> From the court house in the skies,
> And the judge of all the judges,
> May he deem it no surprise
> If I ask him but one favour,
> He may grant it, no one knows,
> Send me back to fair Alberta
> Where the Highwood River flows.
>
> BILL PENDER, DIED 1936
HIGH RIVER, AB, CEMETERY

Here's an example of another modern trend: more and more cowboy and ranching images are appearing in graveyards. Bill Pender was indeed an old rangeland cowboy in southern Alberta. When he died, fellow cowboys and friends chipped in to buy his headstone. The words are his own. He sang them to the tune of "Where the River Shannon Flows."

Heavenly Father, we pause mindful
Of the many blessings you have
Bestowed upon us. We ask that You be
With us at this rodeo and we pray that
You will guide us in the arena of life.
Help us, Lord, to live our lives in
Such a manner that when we make the last
Inevitable ride to the country up there,
Where the grass grows lush green and
Stirrup-high, and the water runs cool,
Clear and deep, that You, as our last judge,
Will tell us that our entry fees are paid.
Amen.

Frank Leon Scout, 1965–1984
Blood Indian Reserve Cemetery, near Standoff, AB

This is the popular "Cowboy's Prayer" that is being used on tombstones in ranching areas all over Canada.

> ## THE COWBOY'S PRAYER
>
> ALMIGHTY FATHER, WE PAUSE, MINDFUL
> OF THE MANY BLESSINGS YOU HAVE
> BESTOWED UPON US. WE ASK THAT YOU BE
> WITH US AT THIS RODEO AND WE PRAY THAT
> YOU WILL GUIDE US IN THE ARENA OF LIFE.
> HELP US LORD, TO LIVE OUR LIVES IN
> SUCH A MANNER THAT WHEN WE MAKE THE LAST
> INEVITABLE RIDE TO THE COUNTRY UP THERE,
> WHERE THE GRASS GROWS LUSH GREEN AND
> STIRRUP – HIGH AND THE WATER RUNS COOL,
> CLEAR AND DEEP, THAT YOU, AS OUR LAST JUDGE,
> WILL TELL US THAT OUR ENTRY FEES ARE PAID.
>
> AMEN.

near Standoff, AB

We roamed the range together,
Undaunted, unfettered so free,
Over trails that are now forgotten,
My brown pony and me.
Over the hills and valleys,
Out where the wild sage grows,
Oh give me back that life so free,
That only a cowboy knows.

Roland Roy Eastman, 1916–1990
Rosemary, AB, Cemetery

Once again, these words were written by the deceased. They share space on his gravemarker with a computer-generated picture of him on his beloved brown pony.

> **Lay my spurs upon my breast**
> **My rope and saddle tree.**
> **And as the boys lay me to rest**
> **Go turn my horses free.**
>
> LINDSAY KITCHNER DOONAN, 1917–1988
> MAPLE CREEK, SK, CEMETERY

Doves are sometimes released at gravesites—or balloons or butterflies—the idea being that as they take flight, so does the soul of the departed. Mr. Doonan, being a rancher, asked instead that his horses run free.

> **He feared God, did nothing mean**
> **Shot straight and stayed clean.**
>
> HULBERT (HULLIE) ORSER, 1897–1981
> EARLVILLE-RUTHERFORD CEMETERY, NEAR PONOKA, AB

This might be called the ultimate western outdoorsman's epitaph. No nonsense, no fancy words, just plain straight talk.

Here's to the things I love the most:
Beautiful horses and lovely ladies.
While I live may I always have
the pleasure to ride
Beautiful horses and to dance
with lovely ladies
When I die may my skin be tanned and
made into a ladies saddle
So that I may always be between the things
I love the most
Beautiful horses and lovely ladies.

DONOVAN GEORGE FLORENCE, 1912–1992
RICHARD, SK, CEMETERY

Donovan Florence was so determined to have his own unique epitaph that he wrote the words above and had them inscribed on a tombstone even before he died. It is not known if his instructions regarding the saddle have been carried out.

> It is a rotten world,
> Artful politicians are its bane.
> Its saving grace is the artlessness of the young
> And the wonders of the sky.
>
> JOHN DEAN, 1850–1943
> ROSS BAY CEMETERY, VICTORIA, BC

This is another man who prepared his gravemarker before he died. He selected the words and had them carved on his marker. Then he decided to add another line—line #2—which had to be squeezed into the space, but he was determined that people understand that politicians were not to be trusted.

> Under this sod lies a sourdough parrot
> Its heart was gold, pure fourteen carat
> Polly now can spread her wings
> Leaving behind all earthly things
> She ranks in fame as our dear departed
> A just reward for being good hearted.
>
> Polly the Parrot, Died 1972
Legend of the North
Carcross, YT, Cemetery

And now for something completely different. This is the epitaph for a parrot who entertained customers at the Carcross hotel for years. She (although they discovered later that Polly was a he) was buried in the local cemetery and marked with a flat tombstone inscribed with the words above.

Death interrupts all that is mortal.

> Mazo de la Roche, 1888–1961
> St. George's Church Cemetery,
> in Sibbald Point Provincial Park, ON

The epitaph for Mazo de la Roche, Canadian author of the Jalna series, tells us what we know only too well. But sometimes death interrupts rudely, with no warning at all. Poor Alexander McKay, below, was simply minding his business, doing his chores, when Death interrupted.

**He was struck down in the
Full vigour of Health and
Hope, by the blow of a horse
And after lingering Five days
In great agony, died, we
Trust a Christian.**

> Alexander McKay, 1800–1819
> Pioneer Cemetery, New Glasgow, NS

Poor Pat, Shot by the Indians

ALBERT EDWARD PATRICK, 1868–1892
FRASER CEMETERY, NEW WESTMINSTER, BC

Horses ran away

JOE YOUNG, 1839–1920
WINDERMERE, BC, CEMETERY

Died from gunshot wounds
Mistaken for a bear

CHARLEY WILLIAM RUDOLF, 1923–1940
ATLIN, BC, CEMETERY

Just in case you were wondering what sent some of the living to the graveyard, here are three sad stories told with a minimum of words on their tombstones.

> Oh, I have slipped
> The surly bonds of earth
> Put out my hand
> And touched the face of God

PILOT OFFICER J. G. MAGEE, DIED 1941
BURIED IN SCOPWICK, ENGLAND

Magee, a pilot and a poet, was with the Royal Canadian Air Force when he was killed in a training accident in England. The words on his grave are from "High Flight," a poem he wrote on the back of a letter to his parents just before he died. Known now as the "pilot's creed," it often appears in shortened form on the gravestones of fliers.

Killed at the Drummond Colliery explosion
While heroically attempting
To save the lives
Of his fellow workmen.

EDWARD BURNS, DIED 1873
DUFF CEMETERY, NEW GLASGOW, NS

There's a whole history book contained in these few lines—the story of Scottish settlers, many of whom came on the now famous Hector, how those settlers worked the mines in Nova Scotia, and how some of those settlers had to die.

Landscape painter
Drowned in Canoe Lake

> Tom Thomson, 1877–1917
> Leith, ON, Cemetery

This, of course, is the famous Canadian painter whose death while canoeing on a lake in northern Ontario is still a major Canadian mystery. The epitaph wastes no words but there's enough there to suggest a larger story.

> To the
> memory
> of a
> proletarian
> Com. S. Berlinic
> Died 27. Feb. 1933
> A victim of
> relief camps
> This monument
> has been erected
> by his comrades
> As a warning
> May 3, 1933.
>
> S. Berlinic, Died 1933
> Prince George, BC, Cemetery

Here's another epitaph that reads like a history book. During the Great Depression of the 1930s, work camps were established for unemployed men, some of whom resented the work forced upon them.

> . . . Full many a man of wealth and power
> Has Died and Gone before
> Who Scorned to Give a Poor Man Bread
> When he Stood at His door
> But Joe took in the Great Unwashed
> Who Shared His Humble Fare
> He Made Their Life a Merry One
> Without a Thought or Care
>
> CHARLES MCKIERNAN, DIED 1889
> MOUNT ROYAL CEMETERY, MONTREAL, QC

Charles McKiernan, a.k.a. "Joe Beef," was known as a champion of the poor in Montreal and he liked nothing better than to upset and aggravate so-called high society. For example, when his first wife died, he had the band play, "The Girl I Left Behind Me" as they left the Mount Royal Cemetery. Sure enough, high society was shocked. Joe Beef loved it. His own funeral was huge, with a miles-long cortège of the "Great Unwashed" following the casket.

> Ye weak, beware! Here lyes the strong
> A victim to his strength.
> He lifted Sixteen Hundred pounds
> And here he lays at length.
>
> Daniel Macdonald, Died 1871
Little Lake Cemetery, Peterborough, ON

Did Mr. Macdonald really die because he lifted too much weight? Yes, indeed he did. For once an epitaph tells us exactly what happened.

> Pathfinder, Pioneer, Miner and Trader
> He was every man's friend and
> Never locked his cabin door.
>
> F. H. "Twelve Foot" Davis, 1820–1900
> Buried on the hills overlooking
> Peace River, AB

As a free trader, Twelve Foot Davis had always had to compete with the Hudson's Bay Company. Before he died, he asked to be interred on the top of the Peace River hills so he could look down and, it is said, piss upon the Hudson's Bay Company in the town below!

... died suddenly at Windsor Castle
December 12, 1894.
Shortly after being sworn in as a member of
Her Majesty's Privy Council
His remains were by command of Her
Majesty Queen Victoria
Borne to Canada by the British man-of-war
Blenheim.

> Sir John S. D. Thompson, 1844–1894
> Prime Minister of Canada 1892–1894
> Holy Cross Cemetery, Halifax, NS

Poor Prime Minister Thompson. Enjoying one of the perks of being a Prime Minister, he was having tea with the Queen in London when he choked on some food and died. The only perk he got was a royal voyage back to Halifax to be buried.

> Duty was the guide of her life
> And the love of her heart
> To her, life was beautiful and good
> She was a benediction to all who knew her
> A breath of the spirit of God
>
> ANNA HARRIET LEONOWENS, 1834–1915
MOUNT ROYAL CEMETERY, MONTREAL, QC

This is the woman who wrote about her life as a teacher for the children of the King of Siam and became the inspiration for the book, stage play, and movie "Anna and the King of Siam." She later moved to be with her daughter in Montreal and died there.

In loving memory of
Mary Anne Cowing
Sept. 23, 1839–Jan. 16, 1908.
Beloved wife of
The Rev. James Robertson, D.D.
Who, denying her heart its claims,
With fidelity, patience and
courage for twenty years
kept her lonely watch over home
and children
That his work for Western Canada might be done.
As she shared his sacrifice,
So she shares his glory.

Mary Anne Cowing, 1839–1908,
Old Kildonan Presbyterian Cemetery,
Winnipeg, MB

The wives of great men are not often remembered so well as is Mary Anne Cowing. A nice example of noblesse oblige.

> The most eloquent voice of the
> Fathers of Confederation
> Born in Carlingford, County Louth, 1825
> Assassinated in Ottawa, 1866.
>
> THOMAS D'ARCY MCGEE 1825–1866
> NOTRE DAME DES NEIGES CEMETERY, MONTREAL, QC

It's not often we see the word "assassinated" on a Canadian gravemarker, but that's certainly what happened to D'Arcy McGee as he stood on his front doorstep late one night in Ottawa. He was a poet and historian as well as a politician, but it was the dastardly politics that did him in.

Gabriel Dumont, 1837–1906

Born in Assiniboia, Rupert's Land
He Won Early Fame as a Buffalo Hunter
About 1868, he founded the Metis Camp
Which Became St. Laurent and in 1873
Became Pres. Of its Local Government

In 1884, He led a Party to Montana
to Bring Back
Louis Riel. He Commanded the
Metis Forces in 1885
And Displayed Considerable Military Ability.
After the Fall of Batoche, He Escaped
to the US.

He Returned Years Later
And Resumed the Life of a Hunter

GABRIEL DUMONT, 1837–1906
BATOCHE, SK, CEMETERY

This is history literally written in stone. All Canadian schoolkids should visit Batoche Cemetery, the site of the last battle of the Northwest Rebellion which was, in fact, one of Canada's civil wars. It was us against us in that battle, and the land issues surrounding the rebellion have never been entirely settled.

In contrast to Dumont's grave, Louis Riel's, in St. Boniface, Manitoba, says very little—just the date of his death by hanging: November 16, 1885.

This promising youth caught the
small-pox at the City of St. John,
Which proved fatal to him
in a few days,
his loss is much lamented
by his relatives and friends.

> WILLIAM SLASON, DIED 1823
> OLD BURYING GROUND, FREDERICTON, NB

We should bring the old word "lamented" back into use. It fits so perfectly into sad situations. See below.

He lived respected
And died lamented,
By all who knew him.

> GEORGE (LAST NAME IS WORN OFF), DIED 1841
> OLD BURYING GROUND, FREDERICTON, NB

Fredericton, NB

Forests were set on fire and hour by hour
They fell and faded and the crackling trunks
Extinguished with a crash and all was black
All earth was but one thought
and that was death.

Ann, wife of John Jackson, and six of their
children aged 15 years to 10 months,
St. Paul's Anglican Cemetery, Chatham, NB

Fires exacted a terrible toll in the early days and the Miramichi fire was one of the worst. Ann Jackson and three of the children perished together in the flames on the night of October 7, 1825. Three more children died in consequence of the fire and "all was black."

> **In this secluded spot**
> **Lie the mortal remains of 5,424 persons**
> **Who flying from Pestilence and Famine**
> **In Ireland in the year 1847 found in America**
> **But a grave.**
>
> Words on a large tombstone on Grosse Île, QC, in the middle of the St. Lawrence River

The words are written there in memory of thousands of immigrants who came to Canada for a new life only to die en route or die on the quarantine island established on Grosse Île. They were victims of the cholera, typhus, and smallpox epidemics of the early 1800s and instead of a new country, they found "but a grave."

> Erected in the memory of
> Samuel Henderson
> Who left his house
> Sound and well July 4
> 1864 and did not return.
> Nor after the most diligent
> Search have any traces
> of him been found. He
> was an humble minded
> Christian. Æ 74 yrs.
> A native of Orkney.
>
> SAMUEL HENDERSON
> KILDONAN PRESBYTERIAN CEMETERY, WINNIPEG, MB

This is a Canadian mystery that's never been solved. Henderson's wife died the following year without ever knowing what had happened to him. He was a city official in his time, and a street has been named for him, but no one knows what happened.

ERECTED
IN MEMORY OF
SAMUEL HENDERSON
Who left his house,
sound & well July 4th
1864 and did not return
nor after the most diligent
search have any traces
of him been found. He
was an humble minded
Christian. Æ 74 yrs.
A native of ORKNEY.

and of
FLORA LIVINGSTONE
his widow
who Died 2, 1865

Winnipeg, MB

> Sacred to the memory of Joseph Jeffs
> Ordy. Seaman H.M.S. Ganges
> who was killed by falling
> from the Mizen Top Oct. 23rd, 1859
> Deeply regretted by his shipmates

JOSEPH JEFFS, DIED 1859
VETERANS CEMETERY, ESQUIMALT, BC

You have to watch for flying golf balls when you visit this cemetery since it's in the middle of a golf course. But once you're safely there, you'll find many stones that relate to the naval history of Canada's west coast, as with the doleful tale of the unfortunate Joseph Jeffs.

> His guitar is dusty
> His house has been sold
> He's jamming in heaven
> With a fiddle of gold.

JOHN JOSEPH LOUIS BERARD, 1945–1988
ST. ANTHONY'S CEMETERY, EDMONTON, AB

"Jamming in heaven" is a long way from "singing with the heavenly choir" but it pretty well means the same thing.

Here reposes Maria Caroline
The generous hearted, high souled,
talented and deeply
Lamented wife of Major Richardson,
Knight of the Military
Order of Saint Ferdinand of the First Class
and Super-Intendent of Police on the
Welland Canal during the
Administration of Lord Metcalfe.
This matchless woman died
Of apoplexy and to the exceeding grief of
her faithfully
Attached husband after a few days illness in
St. Catherines
On the 16th day of August 1845
at the age of 37 years.

BUTLER'S BURYING GROUND, NIAGARA-ON-THE-LAKE, ON

Seems like Major Richardson got as many words as his faithfully attached wife, but never mind, that's how the world turned in 1845. And it's not often you hear the word "apoplexy" nowadays.

Carpe Diem!
Look Thee into Thine Heart and Write.

> Joan Ganong, 1919–1989
> Rural Cemetery, St. Stephen, NB

We should "seize the day" and get down to the business of writing, according to this piece of advice.

Let no man write his epitaph.

> Will O. R. Kemna, 1902–1967
> Queen's Park Cemetery, Calgary, AB

However, there's one thing we shouldn't write, if we take the advice on this man's grave.

The 19th hole

Howard A. Matthews, 1928–1985
St. Marks Cemetery, Hardisty, AB

A golfer's way of saying "Gone Home" or "Safe in the Arms of Jesus."

Goodnight Sweet Prince

Bryce Evans, 1971–1992
Glenwood Memorial Gardens, Sherwood Park, AB

A short and sweet farewell to a young man.

> The Nova Scotia Giant
> Who died at his home
> in St. Anns
> August 6 1863
> aged 38 years
> Height 7 Ft 9 in
> Girth 80 in
> Weight 425 Lbs
> A dutiful son, a loving
> brother, a true friend,
> a loyal subject, a humble
> christian.
>
> Angus McAskill, Died 1863
> Buried near Englishtown, NS

Angus was one of two so-called Canadian giants. The other was Edouard Beaupre of Willow Bunch, Saskatchewan, 1881–1904, who topped Angus at 8'3". Both giants joined freak shows, both hated the experience, and both died young—Beaupre on the road and McAskill back at home in Nova Scotia.

> Not for fame or reward—not for place or rank
> Not lured by ambition—or goaded by necessity
> But in simple obedience to duty
> As he understood it
> Major Norsworthy sacrificed all—suffered all—
> Dared all—and died
>
> Major Edward Cuthbert Norsworthy, 1879–1915
> Memorialized in Ingersoll, ON

You'd be surprised at the number of wars that Canadians have fought in, both on Canadian soil and beyond. Since war service is generally mentioned on gravemarkers, one is able to learn a lot about the history of the world, especially if you do as another Ingersoll military epitaph suggests:

> **Read the history of your country**
> **And understand.**

> Greater love hath no man
> Than this, that a man lay
> Down his life for his friends.

Pte. William Roy Saunders, Died 1919
Died from wounds received at Passchendale,
April 2, 1918, Carbonear, NL, Cemetery

A particularly appropriate epitaph for men who die in combat of some sort or in service to country and community. Private Saunders's grave also includes this reference to war:

> Soldier rest thy warfare o'er.
> Sleep the sleep that knows no wakeing.
> Call to battlefields no more,
> But for you our hearts are breaking.

To Perpetuate
the Name and Fame of
Laura Secord
Who walked alone nearly 20
miles by a circuitous, difficult
and perilous route through woods
and swamps and over miry roads
to warn a British Outpost at
De Cew's Falls of an intended attack
And thereby enabled Lieut. FitzGibbon
on the 24th June, 1813, with less
than 50 men of H.M. 49th regt.,
about 15 militiamen and a small
force of Six Nation and other Indians
under Captains William Johnson Kerr
and Dominique Ducharme, to surprise
and attack the enemy at Beechwoods
(or Beaver Dams), and after a short

engagement to capture Col. Boerstler of the U.S. Army and his entire force of 542 Men with two field pieces.

> Laura Secord, 1775–1868
> Lundy's Lane Cemetery, Niagara Falls, ON

Legend has it that Laura Secord took her cow along to provide a cover for her dangerous mission, but modern-day historians pooh-pooh that idea. They say it would have been too dangerous and slow. So maybe Laura just took a milk pail.

> Then let the worms demand their prey
> The greedy grave my veins consume
> With joy I drop my mouldering clay
> And rest till my Redeemer come
> On Christ my life in death rely
> Secure that I can never die.
>
> MARY BRAGG, 1820–1858
> OLD ANGLICAN CEMETERY, PORT AUX BASQUES, NL

In years gone by, there was much more talk about worms and dust and mouldering clay, but those grisly facts of life (and death) didn't matter so much because, like Mary Bragg, most were secure that they would die on earth only to be resurrected in a better world.

Though bravely sails your bark today
Pale death sits at the prow
And few shall know you ever lived
A hundred years from now

BROWN
HIGH RIVER, AB, CEMETERY

Time has stood as thou dost stand
And viewed the devil as thou dost me
Ere long thou'll be as low as I
And others stand and look on thee.

THOMAS HORNER, 1831–1880
ST. MICHAEL'S ANGLICAN CEMETERY, GRENVILLE, QC

These are epitaphs that remind the living that we too will eventually die. It's a message that's never been particularly popular but can't be avoided in a graveyard, especially when it's presented in such no-nonsense terms.

> We've only one virginity to lose
> And where we lose it
> There our hearts will be.
>
> — Laura Walker, 1890–1914
> Edmonton, AB, Cemetery

You don't often see references to anything that might refer to sex on older grave markers, but this one seems to.

Innisfail, AB

Reader, where will you spend eternity?

> JOHN PENIKETT, DIED 1901
> INNISFAIL, AB, CEMETERY

The answer to that question is not as easy as it used to be when most respondents were religious. For example, the priest who established the first hospital in Dawson City during the gold rush is buried beneath a memorial that includes the Christian assurance

> Here is buried, until it rises up, the body of Father William Judge, died Jan. 16, 1899.

One Old Timer Gone West

> Joe Vallance, 1877–1957
> Chinook, AB, Cemetery

"I'm off to the last round-up"

> Horace A. Greeley, 1858–1935
> Maple Creek, SK, Cemetery

These epitaphs depend on western life for answers. By the way, this Horace Greeley was indeed related to the Horace Greeley who advised, "Go west, young man, go west."

There's got to be a morning after.

> Frank Bower, 1953–1973
> Red Deer, AB, Cemetery

We believe in happy endings
We believe in new beginnings.

> Clifford Kittlitz, 1942–1992
> Moravian Church Cemetery, Bruderheim, AB

An epitaph must convey a lot of meaning in a few words, as these two do. Both could be interpreted to have religious meaning, or not. It's the art of the epitaph.

> For when the one great scorer
> Comes to write against your name
> He writes not that you won or lost
> But how you played the game.
>
> DAVID HUTCHEON ALLAN, 1883–1948
> ESTEVAN, SK, CEMETERY

This epitaph could demonstrate that religion doesn't necessarily reign in the graveyard anymore since God is referred to as "The Great Scorer." It could also demonstrate an original way of speaking about God.

> He who dies with the most toys wins.
>
> BARRY LAWRENCE KAJEWSKI, 1958–1997
> ST. MARGARET'S EAGLE BUTTE CEMETERY,
> NEAR MEDICINE HAT, AB

There's not an angel or religious reference of any sort on this gravemarker. Instead, there are pictures of a fast boat, a fancy car, a big truck, and a loaded bobcat. It's the modern way.

> So that eventually we may lie
> Beside each other in death
> As we lay so happily in life.

MORDECAI RICHLER, 1931–2001
MOUNT ROYAL CEMETERY, MONTREAL, QC

Richler's tombstone is an impressively simple one, a rectangular tablet listing his name and dates plus his wife's name. As is the Jewish custom, there are a number of small stones left on top of the Richler grave, each one indicating a recent visit from friends.

> Have little care that life is brief
> And less that Art is Strong
> Success is in the Silence
> Though Fame is in the Song.

BLISS CARMAN, 1861–1929
FOREST HILL CEMETERY, FREDERICTON, NB

Sometimes, the words of an epitaph can confuse the casual visitor. For instance, does Bliss Carman, one of Canada's best poets ever, wish he had had a little more noise/attention paid to his work?

> Rest lightly on him, O Earth
> He loved you so.

ALDEN NOWLAN, 1933–1983
FOREST HILL CEMETERY, FREDERICTON, NB

There's no mistaking the meaning of the words on the stone of yet another well-known Canadian poet.

> Millicent Milroy, A. M. M. M.
> P. St. Daughter of
> James
> and
> Helen Jane Milroy
> Wife of Edward (VIII)
> Duke of
> Windsor
> 1894–1972
>
> MILLICENT MILROY, 1890–1985
> CAMBRIDGE, ON, CEMETERY

Yes, Millicent Milroy is claiming to be the wife of Edward VIII, the royal who abdicated the British throne to marry Wallis Simpson. The marriage happened during an official visit to Canada, she claimed, and since it's written on her gravemarker, she has the final word.

> **It's not the gales**
> **But the set of the sails**
> **That determines the way you go.**

CHARLES BELL, 1927–1974 AND HAZEL BELL, 1928–1989
MOUNT PLEASANT CEMETERY, TORONTO, ON

Is this a religious message about going to heaven, or is this a secular message about how to live a good life? It could be either, or it could be the words of two people who enjoyed sailing.

A clear conscience makes a soft pillow.

HENRY (HARRY) GLENN DE MILLE, 1914–1968
QUEEN'S PARK CEMETERY, CALGARY, AB

This too could have religious connotations, or it might simply mean that Mr. De Mille lived a good life and his memory is honoured.

T-T-F-N, Daddy-O
We're never apart

M. G. TIM HORTON, 1930–1974
YORK CEMETERY, TORONTO, ON

Yes, this is THE Tim Horton of hockey and doughnut fame. The letters on his grave stand for "Ta Ta For Now." It's a good example of a modern epitaph—not religious but a private meaningful message from family members.

> Warm southern sun shine Kindly here
> Warm southern winds blow softly here
> Green sod above, lie light, lie light,
> Good night, good night.
>
> AILEEN DUFF HOLLOWAY, 1906–1930
> OLDS, AB, CEMETERY

These lovely words have been through a number of adaptations. Written by poet Robert Richardson in 1893, they were changed slightly by Mark Twain for his daughter Susie's epitaph in 1896, and since then have been used, with many variations, on many graves.

Innisfail, AB

> The woods were lovely
> Dark and Deep
> But he had promises to keep
> And miles to go
> 'Fore he could sleep.
>
> Percy Smith, 1916–1981
Fort Nelson, BC, Cemetery

Here is an adaptation of Robert Frost's well-known poem "Stopping By Woods on a Snowy Evening." The Fort Nelson graveyard is surrounded by trees, plain old northern poplars, but indeed the woods are lovely, dark, and deep. A thoughtful goodbye.

> The play is done,
> The play-house dark,
> The player is
> at rest.

> Ida Van Cortland Tavernier, 1855–1924
> Beechwood Cemetery, Ottawa, ON

And finally, there's the dramatic image of curtains closing upon the final act of a play or, as in this case, closing upon a life. No theatrics, just a quiet curtain call, a final bow. Again, it's the art of the epitaph done well.

In Conclusion . . .

Grave words have and have not changed. They are still meant to mark those "whom we have loved and lost awhile"—to quote one of the epitaphs. They still express our grief at the loss. They still remind us of those who have gone before. But the use of religious references is less prevalent today, which means that overall the epitaphs are shorter, less poetic, and more dependent on images of life on earth rather than life in Heaven. In other words, many of them have changed from public expressions of grief and belief to private messages or no messages at all.

Indeed, with the trend more and more toward cremation, many of us are not marked at all anymore. Our ashes have been scattered on a mountaintop, interred in a private grove of trees, or forgotten in a drawer, which means that cemeteries are no longer the sole repository of those who have gone before. That, in turn, means that future generations may not be able to find the stones of their ancestors. It's a contradiction, but there's something about a stone with words on it that makes a life seem real. A schoolchild, for example, will believe and remember the history of the North West Mounted Police when he or she stands in front of the tombstone in Calgary's Union Cemetery that reads: "Crossed the Plains in 1874 as

Inspector in the Original North West Mounted Police." That stone belongs to Captain Sir Cecil Edward Denny and he truly was one of those men who put on a red jacket, rode a horse across the plains, and figured out how to be a police force in western Canada. It's a great story.

But if modern trends continue and we don't have stones with words upon them, how will future generations find us and say, "This is my grandmother, this is the mapmaker that found the Pacific, this is a poor woman who died in childbirth?" How will the people who came before be real to us? Or does it matter anymore? So many things have already changed. Why shouldn't dying and remembering be different too? Maybe it's simply time to adjust to this brave new world and admit we don't need epitaphs or tombstones out there in the graveyard to remember.

Or maybe we do. Epitaphs along with names and dates on tombstones are one way not to be forgotten. Watch people in a graveyard and they will pause before a stone, read the names, winkle out as much information as they can from the words and dates, and then say, "I wonder what this person did? I wonder what happened?" And for one teeny tiny moment, the deceased is remembered as we pass by.

Remember me as you pass by
So as you are, So once was I.

Niagara Falls, ON

Index

Anon., Charlottetown, PEI, 42

mass grave, Grosse Île, QC, 81

[no last name], George, Fredericton, NB, 78, 79

A

Allan, David Hutcheon, Estevan, SK, 101

Allen, Martha, Oshawa, ON, 31

Anderson, Catherine, Ormstown, QC, 42

B

Baker, Frank Russell "Russ", Fort St. James, BC, 16

Bartlett, Joseph, Brigus, NL, 32

Beaupre, Edouard, Willow Bunch, SK, 89

Begley, Samuel, Aylwin, QC, 46

Bell, Charles and Hazel, Toronto, ON, 105

Berard, John Joseph Louis, Edmonton, AB, 85

Berlinic, S., Prince George, BC, 68

Biggar, Rebecca G., Niagara Falls, ON, 35

"Big Jack," Edam, SK, 52, 53

Bower, Frank, Red Deer, AB, 100

Bragg, Mary, Port aux Basques, NL, 94

Brodair, Petter D., Pictou, NS, 34

Brown, High River, AB, 95

Burns, Edward, New Glasgow, NS, 66

C

Cameron, Senator Donald and Stella Mary, Banff, AB, 24

Carman, Bliss, Fredericton, NB, 103

Carter, Wilf, 7

Chapman, Nellie, Vernon, BC, 8, 9

Clephane, George, Fergus, ON, 21

Connell, Harriet Elizabeth, Okotoks, AB, 39

Cowing, Mary Anne, Winnipeg, MB, 74

Coyne, Michael, Calgary, AB, 44

Custer, George Armstrong, 36, 37

Czemeres, Esther, Fort Qu'Appelle, SK, 7

D

Davis, F. H. "Twelve Foot," Peace River, AB, 71

Dean, John, Victoria, BC, 61

de la Roche, Mazo, Sibbald Point Provincial Park, ON, 63

De Mille, Henry (Harry) Glenn, Calgary, AB, 106

Denny, Sir Cecil Edward, Calgary, AB, 113

Devore, Roy William, Edmonton, AB, 50

Doonan, Lindsay Kitchner, Maple Creek, SK, 59

Dumont, Gabriel, Batoche, SK, 76, 77

E

Eastman, Roland Roy, Rosemary, AB, 58

Edward VIII, 104

Elliott, Everett Edward, Halifax, NS, 47

Evans, Bryce, Sherwood Park, AB, 88

F

Fedora, Constance and William, Pleasant Home, MB, 3

Ferguson, Duncan McIntyre, 6

Fields, W. C., 4

Fleming, Sir Sandford, Ottawa, 20

Florence, Donovan George, Richard, SK, 60

Frost, Robert, 110

G

Ganong, Joan, St. Stephen, NB, 87

Greeley, Horace A., Maple Creek, SK, 99

H

Hancocks, Kraig, Tappen, BC, 2

Harrold, George Kenneth, Fort Nelson, BC, 16

Henderson, Samuel, Winnipeg, MB, 82, 83

Hiscock, Jane, Trinity, NL, 15

Holloway, Aileen Duff, Olds, AB, 108, *109*

Horner, Thomas, Grenville, QC, 95

Horton, M. G. Tim, Toronto, ON, 107

Hunter, Harold Gilray, Ingersoll, ON, *vi*

I

Ireland, Alex, Moose Jaw, SK, 23

J

Jackson, Ann, and children, Chatham, NB, 80

Jeffs, Joseph, Esquimalt, BC, 84

Judge, William, Dawson City, YT, 98

K

Kajewski, Barry Lawrence, near Medicine Hat, AB, 101

Kemna, Will O. R., Calgary, AB, 87

Kidney, Forest and Maud, Banff, AB, 25

Kittlitz, Clifford, Bruderheim, AB, 100

L

Lebeuf, Edwin, near Spirit River, AB, 40, *41*

Leonowens, Anna Harriet, Montreal, QC, 73

Limpert, Gladys, Delia, AB, 4

Longworth, Agnes, Charlottetown, PEI, 48

M

Macdonald, Daniel, Peterborough, ON, 70

Mackay, Eric Grant, Calgary, AB, 54

Mackay family, St. John, NB, 6

Macleod, son of Rev. Norman, Pictou, NS, 33

Magee, J. G., Scopwick, England, 65

Marshall, Kory Dale, Delia, AB, 45

Martel, Louis, Edmonton, AB, 5

Matthews, Howard A., Hardisty, AB, 88

McAlpine, John, Three Hills, AB, 36, 37

McAskill, Angus, near Englishtown, NS, 89

McCurdy, John Alexander Douglas, Baddeck, NS, 38

McDonald, John Donald, Victoria, BC, 54

McEdward, Margaret, South Lancaster, ON, 20

McGee, Thomas D'Arcy, Montreal, QC, 75

McKay, Alexander, New Glasgow, NS, 63

McKiernan, Charles, Montreal, QC, 69

McQuaig, Malcolm and Margery (Clark), Pictou, NS, 10

Miller, Eva Leona Hedges, Olds, AB, 33

Milroy, Millicent, Cambridge, ON, 104

N

Norsworthy, Edward Cuthbert, Ingersoll, ON, 90

Nowlan, Alden, Fredericton, NB, 103

O

Orser, Hulbert (Hullie), near Ponoka, AB, 59

P

Patrick, Albert Edward, New Westminster, BC, 64

Pender, Bill, High River, AB, 55

Penikett, John, Innisfail, AB, 97, 98

Pennington, Peter, Sarnia, ON, 30

Phillips, Harold Huntington, Dalemead, AB, 38

Pierce, William, Picton, ON, 18, 19

Pollock, Mary Ann, Sintaluta, SK, 27

Polly the Parrot, Carcross, YT, 62

R

Ratcliff, William Dennis, Sundre, AB, 17

Red Crow, Annie Iron, Standoff, AB, 51

Richardson, Maria Caroline, Niagara-on-the-Lake, ON, 86

Richardson, Robert, 108

Richler, Mordecai, Montreal, QC, 102

Riel, Louis, St. Boniface, MB, 77

Rudolf, Charley William, Atlin, BC, 64

S

Saunders, William Roy, Carbonear, NL, 91

Scout, Frank Leon, near Standoff, AB, 56, 57

Secord, Laura, Niagara Falls, ON, 92, 93, *114*

Sharpe, Kathleen, Millarville, AB, viii

Shaw, Marjorie Edith, Victoria, BC, 11

Sheahan, Catherine, Old Chelsea, QC, 14

Sheppard, Freddy, Wetaskiwin, AB, 40

Shirt, Keysoos McLean, Fort Vermilion, AB, 51

Sibbald, Andrew S., Banff, AB, 52

Simpson, Wallis, 104

Slason, William, Fredericton, NB, 78

Smith, Mary, Montreal, QC, 22

Smith, Percy, Fort Nelson, BC, 110

Strang, Ann, Cambridge, ON, 12, *13*

Stoughton, Howard, Barryvale, ON, 26

Sumner, Daisy, Yale, BC, 52

T

Tavernier, Ida Van Cortland, Ottawa, ON, 111

Taylor, Lorren, Red Deer, AB, 18

Thompson, Sir John S. D., Halifax, NS, 72

Thompson, Thomas, Toronto, ON, 1

Thomson, Tom, Leith, ON, 67

Thorne, John Reginald, Toronto, ON, 49

Townsend, Jane, Wakefield, QC, 43

Twain, Mark, 108

V

Vallance, Joe, Chinook, AB, 99

W

Walker, Laura, Edmonton, AB, 96

Winslow, Hannah, Fredericton, NB, 28

Y

Yeats, William Butler, 44

Young, Joe, Windermere, BC, 64

Nancy Millar, an Albertan born and bred, has had a lot of lives—teacher, television news anchor for CBC, newspaper columnist for *The Red Deer Advocate* and *The Calgary Herald*, and most recently author of six books, including two others on graveyards: *Remember Me as You Pass By* and *Once Upon a Tomb*. In between and always, she's a graveyard explorer, and that's where these epitaphs have come from.

N

Norsworthy, Edward Cuthbert, Ingersoll, ON, 90

Nowlan, Alden, Fredericton, NB, 103

O

Orser, Hulbert (Hullie), near Ponoka, AB, 59

P

Patrick, Albert Edward, New Westminster, BC, 64

Pender, Bill, High River, AB, 55

Penikett, John, Innisfail, AB, 97, 98

Pennington, Peter, Sarnia, ON, 30

Phillips, Harold Huntington, Dalemead, AB, 38

Pierce, William, Picton, ON, 18, 19

Pollock, Mary Ann, Sintaluta, SK, 27

Polly the Parrot, Carcross, YT, 62

R

Ratcliff, William Dennis, Sundre, AB, 17

Red Crow, Annie Iron, Standoff, AB, 51

Richardson, Maria Caroline, Niagara-on-the-Lake, ON, 86

Richardson, Robert, 108

Richler, Mordecai, Montreal, QC, 102

Riel, Louis, St. Boniface, MB, 77

Rudolf, Charley William, Atlin, BC, 64

S

Saunders, William Roy, Carbonear, NL, 91

Scout, Frank Leon, near Standoff, AB, 56, *57*

Secord, Laura, Niagara Falls, ON, 92, 93, *114*

Sharpe, Kathleen, Millarville, AB, viii

Shaw, Marjorie Edith, Victoria, BC, 11

Sheahan, Catherine, Old Chelsea, QC, 14

Sheppard, Freddy, Wetaskiwin, AB, 40

Shirt, Keysoos McLean, Fort Vermilion, AB, 51

Sibbald, Andrew S., Banff, AB, 52

Simpson, Wallis, 104

Slason, William, Fredericton, NB, 78

Smith, Mary, Montreal, QC, 22

Smith, Percy, Fort Nelson, BC, 110

Strang, Ann, Cambridge, ON, 12, *13*

Stoughton, Howard, Barryvale, ON, 26

Sumner, Daisy, Yale, BC, 52

T

Tavernier, Ida Van Cortland, Ottawa, ON, 111

Taylor, Lorren , Red Deer, AB, 18

Thompson, Sir John S. D., Halifax, NS, 72

Thompson, Thomas, Toronto, ON, 1

Thomson, Tom, Leith, ON, 67

Thorne, John Reginald, Toronto, ON, 49

Townsend, Jane, Wakefield, QC, 43

Twain, Mark, 108

V

Vallance, Joe, Chinook, AB, 99

W

Walker, Laura, Edmonton, AB, 96

Winslow, Hannah, Fredericton, NB, 28

Y

Yeats, William Butler, 44

Young, Joe, Windermere, BC, 64

Nancy Millar, an Albertan born and bred, has had a lot of lives—teacher, television news anchor for CBC, newspaper columnist for *The Red Deer Advocate* and *The Calgary Herald*, and most recently author of six books, including two others on graveyards: *Remember Me as You Pass By* and *Once Upon a Tomb*. In between and always, she's a graveyard explorer, and that's where these epitaphs have come from.